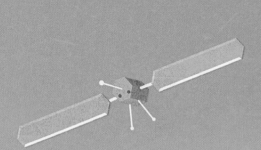

D1457146

THIS IS A CARLTON BOOK

First published in this edition in 2018
by Carlton Books Limited,
an imprint of the Carlton Publishing Group,
20 Mortimer Street, London W1T 3JW

Text and design copyright
© Carlton Books Limited 2015

ISBN: 978-1-78312-393-3

All rights reserved. This book is sold subject to
the condition that it may not be reproduced,
stored in a retrieval system or transmitted in any
form or by any means, electronic, mechanical,
photocopying, recording or otherwise, without
the publisher's prior consent.

A catalogue record for this book is
available from the British Library.

Printed in Dubai

10 9 8 7 6 5 4 3 2 1

Executive Editor: Bryony Davies
Design Manager: Emily Clarke
Design: Ceri Hurst
Production: Nicola Davey

To Kamini, Vikas and Sachin – R.P.

AMAZING SPACE

GO ON A JOURNEY TO THE EDGE OF THE UNIVERSE

WRITTEN BY RAMAN PRINJA
ILLUSTRATED BY JOHN HERSEY

CARLTON KIDS

CONTENTS

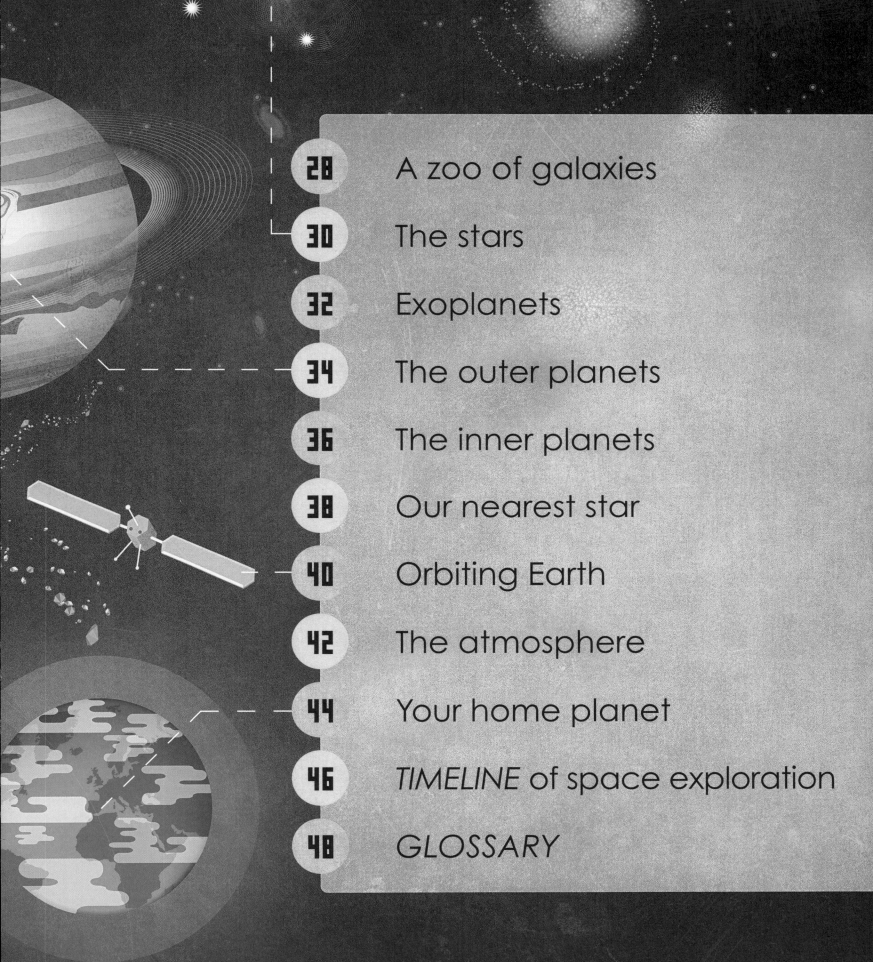

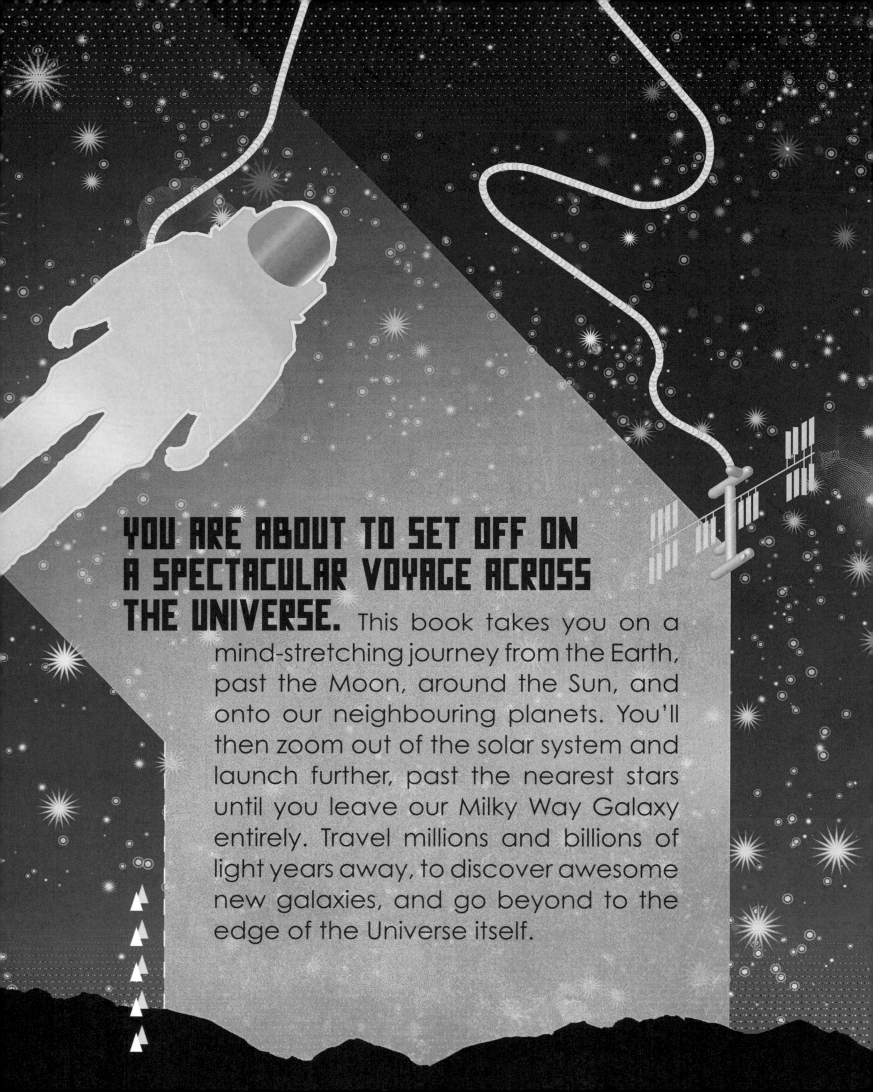

YOU ARE ABOUT TO SET OFF ON A SPECTACULAR VOYAGE ACROSS THE UNIVERSE. This book takes you on a mind-stretching journey from the Earth, past the Moon, around the Sun, and onto our neighbouring planets. You'll then zoom out of the solar system and launch further, past the nearest stars until you leave our Milky Way Galaxy entirely. Travel millions and billions of light years away, to discover awesome new galaxies, and go beyond to the edge of the Universe itself.

You'll then start a whole new voyage of discovery as you return from deepest space. Pick up some incredible facts about the Universe on the journey home. Learn about mysterious dark matter and energy that fills the Universe, and chart the life cycles of stars. Pass black holes and exploding supergiant stars on the way back into our solar system. Get weighed on other planets and check out their weather forecasts. Spend time with astronauts on the International Space Station, before finally flying back through Earth's atmosphere and back home.

The Universe is incredibly huge. Even light, which travels faster than anything else (with a speed of 300,000 kilometres per second) takes 93 billion years to move across the Universe that we can see. But the Universe has not always been the same size. About 14 billion years ago it was all collected into just one tiny point in space. Since then, it has been growing outwards at very high speeds, inflating like a giant balloon. So the vastness of space we see today is billions of times greater than it was when the Universe was first born. Our home planet may seem extremely large to us, but you'll soon discover as we start our cosmic voyage, that it is just a tiny speck in an enormous expanding Universe.

PLANET EARTH

LOOK AROUND YOU.

Wherever you are, whoever you are, you are on planet Earth.
Earth is the only planet we know of that has life and liquid water on its surface.
It spins on its axis once a day, making the Sun, Moon and stars rise and set. The Earth also glides in an orbit around the Sun once per year, giving us seasons. It is our home in our solar system, from which we can see out into the Universe.

» About **70%** of the Earth's surface is covered in water and oceans.

Earth is an active planet,
with powerful hurricanes, volcanoes
erupting hot lava, and earthquakes that shake the
land. The continents we live on are slowly moving, forming
mountains and deep valleys. Warmed by the Sun, there
are about 9 million different forms of life on Earth today.

OUR PLANET IS 4.5 BILLION YEARS OLD, and has seen many different types of living creatures. Life on Earth began with single-cell organisms, and burst into a diverse multitude in an event called the 'Cambrian explosion' about 500 million years ago. Dinosaurs, woolly mammoths and sabre-toothed tigers are some of the fascinating creatures that lived on Earth but which are now extinct.

In their place, **over 7 billion humans now live on Earth.**

ABOVE EARTH

Above its surface, Earth is wrapped in a blanket of air called **THE ATMOSPHERE.**

It is held in place by Earth's gravity and keeps the temperature down below comfortable for us. Nearly three-quarters of the atmosphere is made of nitrogen gas, and most of the rest is the oxygen that we breathe.

Earth's atmosphere gets thinner and thinner the higher you go.

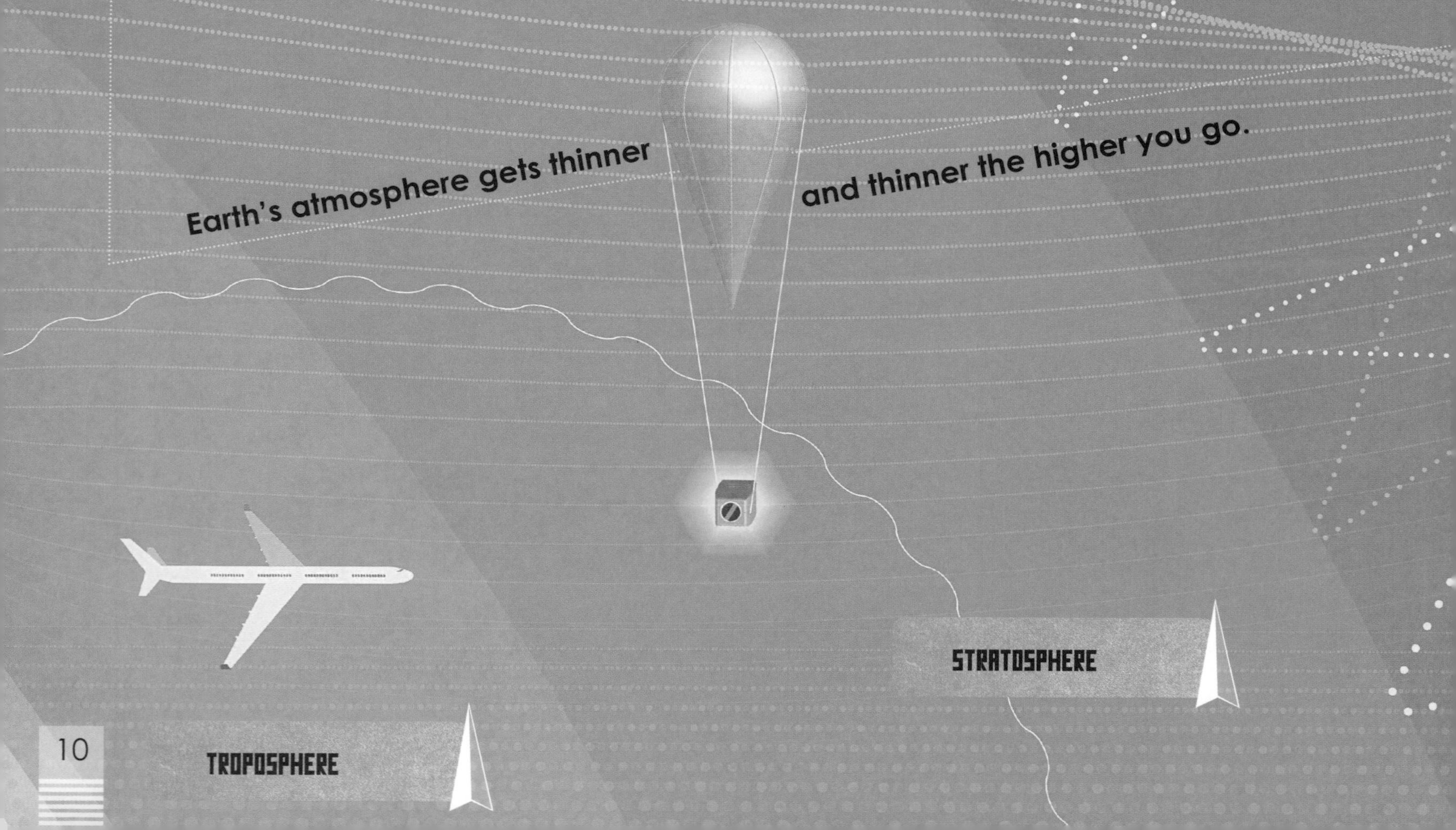

STRATOSPHERE

TROPOSPHERE

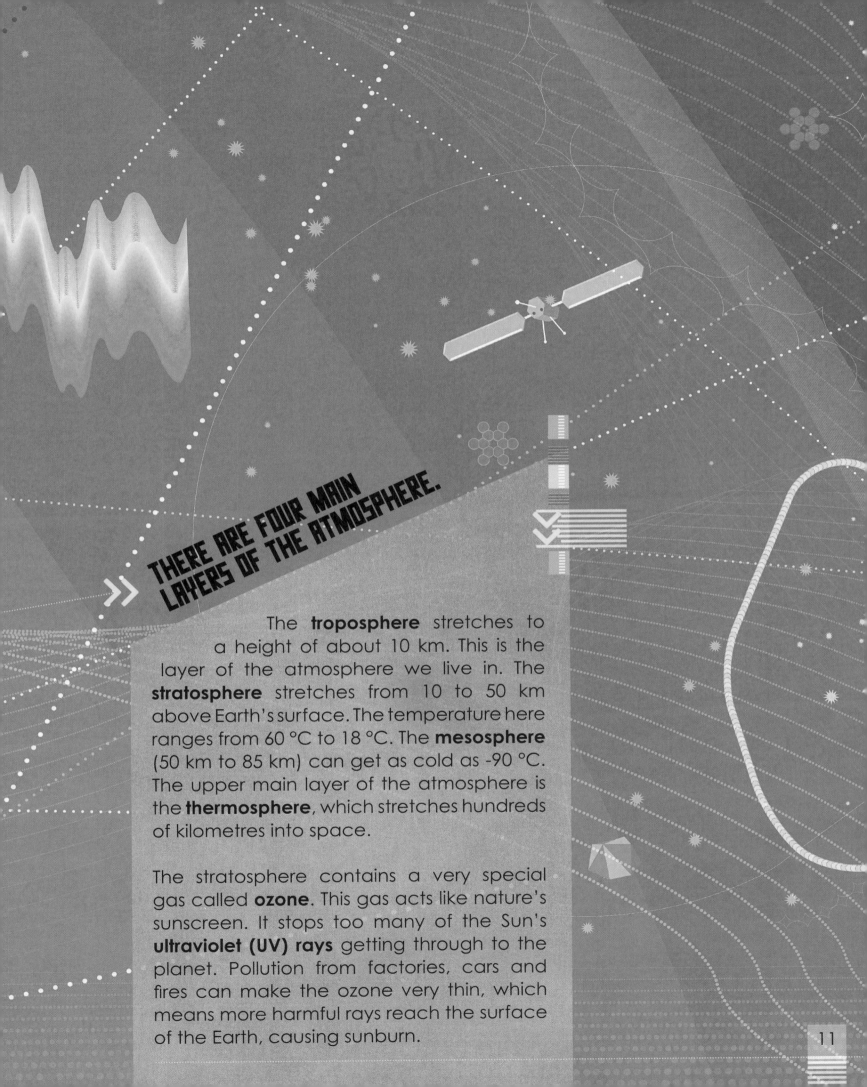

THERE ARE FOUR MAIN LAYERS OF THE ATMOSPHERE.

The **troposphere** stretches to a height of about 10 km. This is the layer of the atmosphere we live in. The **stratosphere** stretches from 10 to 50 km above Earth's surface. The temperature here ranges from 60 °C to 18 °C. The **mesosphere** (50 km to 85 km) can get as cold as -90 °C. The upper main layer of the atmosphere is the **thermosphere**, which stretches hundreds of kilometres into space.

The stratosphere contains a very special gas called **ozone**. This gas acts like nature's sunscreen. It stops too many of the Sun's **ultraviolet (UV) rays** getting through to the planet. Pollution from factories, cars and fires can make the ozone very thin, which means more harmful rays reach the surface of the Earth, causing sunburn.

INHABITING SPACE

At a distance of **384,000 km**, the Moon is much further away from Earth than the International Space Station.

INTERNATIONAL SPACE STATION (ISS)

>> Several astronauts usually live and work together in the **International Space Station (ISS)**. They carry out scientific experiments both inside and outside the ISS. Supplies, such as food and water, are sent to them from Earth using rockets. Sometimes the astronauts do spacewalks outside the space station, wearing special suits that keep them warm and protect them from the Sun.

While a rocket can take astronauts to the ISS in just 6 hours, in the late 1960s and early 1970s it took 3 days for the Apollo missions to fly astronauts to the Moon!

The Moon's surface is covered with rocks and dark grey dust. There are many large craters on the Moon that formed when comets and asteroids crashed there billions of years ago. Some of the ice from these comets is still on the Moon's surface today! There is no water, atmosphere, wind or life on the Moon.

For a spacecraft to be launched into orbit around Earth, it needs to travel at an amazing 40,000 km/h. Thousands of man-made satellites orbit just a few hundred kilometres above the Earth, as do the Hubble Space Telescope and the ISS.

THE SUN

THE SUN IS OUR NEAREST STAR

and the centre of our solar system. Like all stars, the Sun is a gigantic ball of hydrogen and helium gas. Nuclear energy generated in the Sun's core keeps it hot and shining.

Our Sun is 150 MILLION KM from Earth.

Our Sun looks bigger and brighter than the other stars in the night sky because it is much closer to us. **The next nearest star to the Sun is nearly 270,000 times further away!**

Sometimes there are tremendous explosions on the surface of the Sun called **FLARES.**

Huge blasts of radiation and gas burst out of the Sun during a flare. When this electrified gas strikes Earth, it can cause beautiful light shows in our planet's atmosphere called **aurorae.** Flares and other storms from the Sun can also harm satellites and astronauts when they are in orbit around the Earth.

OUR SOLAR SYSTEM

THERE ARE
8 PLANETS

in our solar system, as well as thousands of smaller objects, such as moons, comets and asteroids. It formed around 5 billion years ago out of a huge cloud of swirling gas and dust. The planets closest to the Sun are rocky, with solid surfaces you could stand on.

VENUS is about the size of the Earth, but it is wrapped in a very thick atmosphere. It traps enough heat to make Venus's surface so hot it could melt lead!

MERCURY is closest to the Sun and the smallest planet. Its grey surface is covered in craters, a lot like Earth's moon.

You can't see Earth because you're standing on it!

PHOBOS

DEIMOS

MARS **is the last inner planet.** It is about half the size of Earth and has two small moons called Phobos and Deimos. The surface of Mars is red because of iron in its rocks, which have rusted there. Mars had lots of liquid water millions of years ago, but it has all evaporated away now. There is an incredible 25-km-high volcanic mountain called Olympus Mons on Mars!

Between Mars and the outer planets lies a huge swarm of asteroids, called the 'asteroid belt'. Asteroids are chunks of rock and metal that also circle the Sun. Thousands of larger asteroids have been discovered in this belt, and it is likely to contain millions of 1-kilometre-sized asteroids that we can't see from Earth.

JUPITER is the king of the planets. We can see coloured layers of clouds high in its atmosphere that make swirling patterns as the planet spins around very quickly. There is also a giant storm called the Great Red Spot. It is twice the size of the Earth and has been raging for more than 300 years.

NEPTUNE is so far away it takes about 165 Earth years to complete an orbit around the Sun. It has the strongest winds anywhere in the solar system.

URANUS is smaller than Saturn and is blue because of methane gas in its atmosphere. It spins on its side and has vertical rings.

SATURN has beautiful bright rings made of chunks of ice. The rings are more than 280,000 km across but only 1 km thick. It has 62 moons including Titan, the only known satellite to have its own atmosphere.

OUTSIDE THE ASTEROID BELT

Giant planets formed beyond the asteroid belt, where temperatures are much lower. They are mostly made of hydrogen and helium, and have rings around them and dozens of moons. These giant planets are mostly made of liquefied gas. They don't have a surface so you could never land on one!

Beyond Neptune lie huge numbers of small, icy worlds including the dwarf planets Pluto, Haumea, Makemake and Eris. At almost 120 times the distance between the Earth and the Sun, we reach the solar system's edge, called the heliopause. Beyond it we no longer feel the effects of the Sun, **and we are heading into the space between the stars.**

SUPER STARS

LOOKING DEEPER AND DEEPER INTO SPACE,
a great variety of stars come into view.

Some of the stars are much larger than the Sun and shine far more brilliantly. While some are hundreds of times larger than the Sun, others are far smaller and dimmer. They are also very far apart from each other. The next nearest star to the Sun is almost 4 light years (40 trillion km) away and there are 100 billion stars beyond that in our galaxy.

STAR BIRTH NURSERY

Just like human beings, stars have their own life cycles, but they take billions of years to form. SOMEWHERE IN SPACE TODAY WHILE SOME STARS ARE BEING BORN, OTHERS ARE DYING.

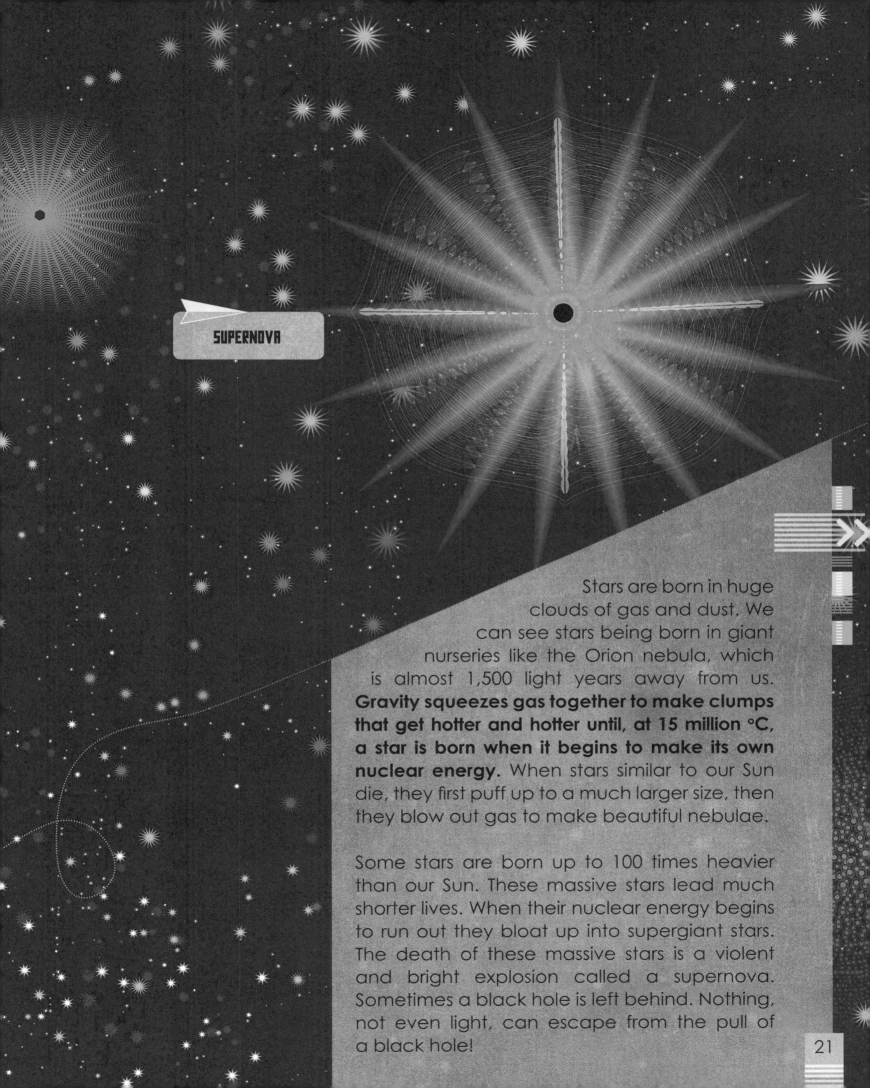

SUPERNOVA

Stars are born in huge clouds of gas and dust. We can see stars being born in giant nurseries like the Orion nebula, which is almost 1,500 light years away from us. **Gravity squeezes gas together to make clumps that get hotter and hotter until, at 15 million °C, a star is born when it begins to make its own nuclear energy.** When stars similar to our Sun die, they first puff up to a much larger size, then they blow out gas to make beautiful nebulae.

Some stars are born up to 100 times heavier than our Sun. These massive stars lead much shorter lives. When their nuclear energy begins to run out they bloat up into supergiant stars. The death of these massive stars is a violent and bright explosion called a supernova. Sometimes a black hole is left behind. Nothing, not even light, can escape from the pull of a black hole!

21

GROUPS OF GALAXIES

ALMOST ALL STARS IN THE UNIVERSE BELONG TO GALAXIES.

The Universe has more than 100 billion galaxies, with each galaxy containing around 100 billion stars, and probably billions of planets too. It takes a gigantic universe to fit in all this matter and still leave huge empty regions of space between them! Looking millions of light years away we can see galaxies everywhere.

Some galaxies are BEAUTIFUL SPIRALS;

Most of the galaxies in the Universe exist in groups, bound together by the force of gravity. Our galaxy is part of a local group of about 50 galaxies. Sometimes galaxies in a group get too close and smash into each other. These powerful cosmic collisions can make larger galaxies and lots of new stars.

others are shaped like **SPHERES** or **ELLIPSES**.

On an even larger scale, we can see that different groups of galaxies are also tied together by gravity. Our local group of galaxies is linked with many others to form a supercluster of hundreds of galaxies that stretch 100 million light years across. Looking as far as 300 million light years into space we can see other superclusters made up of thousands of galaxies.

THE BIG BANG

AT THE EDGE OF THE UNIVERSE WE CAN SEE BACK IN TIME TO ITS VERY BEGINNING.

The Universe began in a Big Bang about 13.8 billion years ago. It started as an incredibly hot and dense bubble thousands of times smaller than a pinhead! Time, space and matter all began with the Big Bang, though we don't know what caused it.

VERY QUICKLY THE UNIVERSE STARTED TO GROW – AND IT IS STILL EXPANDING TODAY.

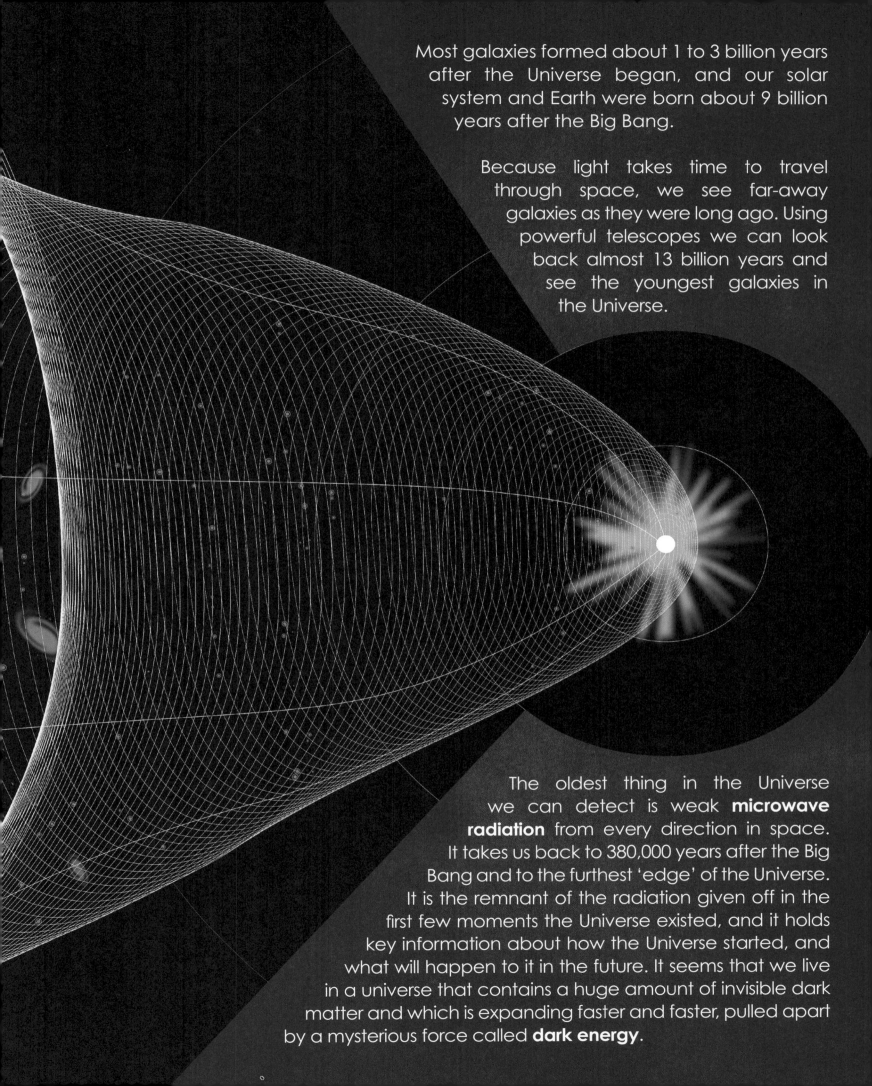

Most galaxies formed about 1 to 3 billion years after the Universe began, and our solar system and Earth were born about 9 billion years after the Big Bang.

Because light takes time to travel through space, we see far-away galaxies as they were long ago. Using powerful telescopes we can look back almost 13 billion years and see the youngest galaxies in the Universe.

The oldest thing in the Universe we can detect is weak **microwave radiation** from every direction in space. It takes us back to 380,000 years after the Big Bang and to the furthest 'edge' of the Universe. It is the remnant of the radiation given off in the first few moments the Universe existed, and it holds key information about how the Universe started, and what will happen to it in the future. It seems that we live in a universe that contains a huge amount of invisible dark matter and which is expanding faster and faster, pulled apart by a mysterious force called **dark energy.**

THE EDGE OF THE UNIVERSE

BIG BANG
13.8 billion years ago

AFTERGLOW
380,000 years after Big Bang

FIRST STARS FORMED
180 million years after Big Bang

GALAXIES FORMED WITH STARS AND PLANETS

RUNAWAY UNIVERSE PUSHED APART BY DARK ENERGY

THE UNIVERSE IS MADE OF:

5% Ordinary matter
Stars, galaxies, planets, dust and gas

24% Cold dark matter
Made of mysterious particles much smaller than an atom

71% Dark energy
A mysterious force that is making the Universe expand faster and faster

FUTURE UNIVERSE

Here are some theories of what might happen to the Universe in the far future.

CRUNCH
It would stop expanding in the future and start to shrink down.

CONTINUE FOREVER
It would carry on slowly expanding forever.

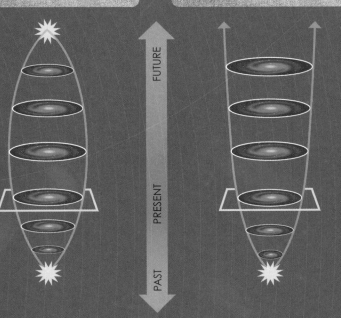

FUTURE

PRESENT

PAST

RUNAWAY UNIVERSE
Today we think that the Universe is expanding more and more quickly.

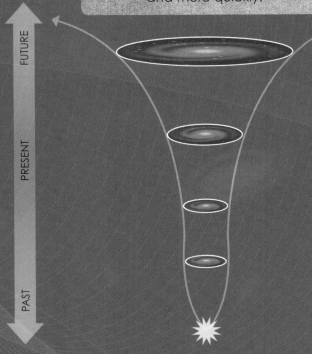

FUTURE

PRESENT

PAST

COSMIC CALENDAR

Imagine the **13.8-billion-year history of the Universe** scaled down to one calendar year.

JANUARY	**1ST**	Big Bang
FEBRUARY		
MARCH		
APRIL		
MAY	**1ST**	Milky Way galaxy forms
JUNE		
JULY		
AUGUST		
SEPTEMBER	**9TH**	Origin of the solar system
	14TH	Earth forms
OCTOBER		
NOVEMBER	**15TH**	First life cells on Earth
DECEMBER	**19TH**	First land plants appear on Earth
	25TH	First dinosaurs
	29TH	Dinosaurs wiped out by comet crash

The last 20 seconds of the year are all of human civilization!

A ZOO OF GALAXIES

OUR POSITION IN OUR GALAXY

SOLAR SYSTEM

SUPERMASSIVE BLACK HOLE

LIGHT YEAR DISTANCES

Light year = distance travelled by light in a year = 9,460,000,000,000 km (9.5 trillion km)

Light moves at a speed of 300,000 km per second!

The Sun takes **220 MILLION YEARS** to complete one orbit around the galaxy.

There may be **100,000,000,000 STARS** in our galaxy!
There may be 15 billion Earth-like planets too.

ALL SORTS OF GALAXIES

ELLIPTICAL GALAXIES
Ball- and egg-shaped

SPIRAL GALAXIES
Disc with bulge in centre
and spiral arms

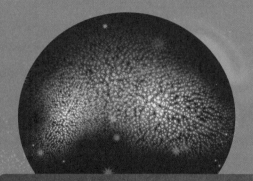

IRREGULARS
No clear shape

PERCENTAGE OF TYPES OF NEARBY GALAXIES

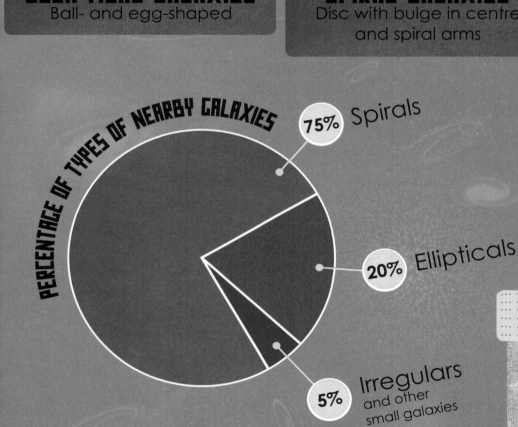

75% Spirals

20% Ellipticals

5% Irregulars
and other
small galaxies

5 million light years

LARGEST GALAXY

Largest known galaxy **IC 1101** is
over 5 million light years across –
more than 50 Milky Way galaxies
could fit across it.

NEAREST GALAXY

The next nearest large spiral galaxy to the Milky Way is called the
Andromeda galaxy. It is the most distant thing we can see with our
naked eyes – but you need a very dark site, and clear night! Andromeda
is **2.3 million light years away from Earth** – but it's heading towards us!
The two galaxies will COLLIDE in about 4 billion years!

THE STARS

Just like human beings, stars have their own life cycles, but they can shine for billions of years.

LIFE CYCLE OF A STAR

Gas cloud

Sun-like star → Red giant → Planetary nebula → White dwarf

Massive star → Supergiant → Supernova → Black hole / Neutron star

LARGEST AND MOST POWERFUL KNOWN STARS

The **largest known stars** are almost 1,500 times wider than the Sun. Examples of these supergiant stars are **UY Scuti**, **W26** and **KY Cygni** – more than 3 billion Suns would fit inside these enormous stars.

The most **powerful star*** called **R136a1** is 165,000 light years away. It is more than 35 times the mass of the Sun and is 8,700,000 times more powerful than the Sun.

* Here power refers to the total light given off.

BLACK HOLES

A massive object like a star or galaxy in space curves the space around it.

All the mass is squeezed into a tiny volume. Space is now so curved that matter cannot escape.

There may be 1,000,000,000,000,000,000,000,000 STARS
(one thousand billion trillion) in the Universe!

Here are some star constellations visible from Earth:

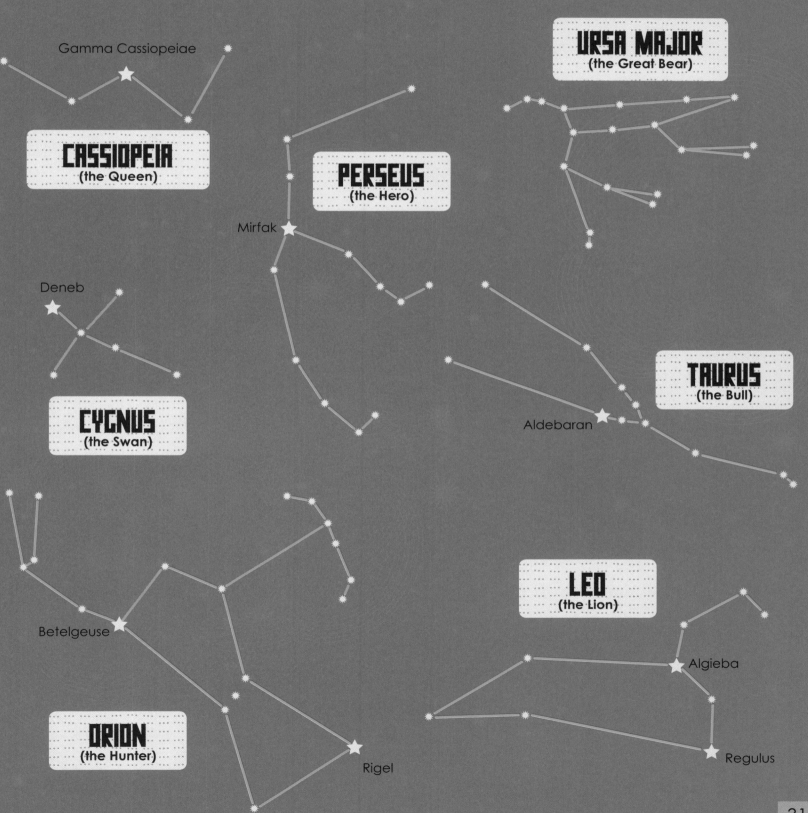

Gamma Cassiopeiae

URSA MAJOR
(the Great Bear)

CASSIOPEIA
(the Queen)

PERSEUS
(the Hero)

Mirfak

Deneb

TAURUS
(the Bull)

Aldebaran

CYGNUS
(the Swan)

Betelgeuse

LEO
(the Lion)

Algieba

ORION
(the Hunter)

Rigel

Regulus

EXOPLANETS

Exoplanets, also called extrasolar planets are planets that orbit other stars beyond our solar system.

There are currently nearly **4,000** confirmed exoplanets going around other stars.

Astronomers think there may be at least **100 BILLION EXOPLANETS IN OUR MILKY WAY GALAXY.**

LAUNCHED ON 7 MARCH 2009, the **Kepler Space Telescope** has discovered thousands of possible exoplanets in our Galaxy.

x5

THERE ARE MANY DIFFERENT TYPES OF KNOWN EXOPLANETS,

including **Rocky Earth-like planets, Super Earths** that are 5 times more massive than Earth, **Ocean planets** covered in water, and **Hot Jupiters** – giant gas planets that are much hotter than Jupiter or Saturn.

55 CANCRI E is an incredibly hot world that **zooms around its star every 18 hours**. It orbits about 25 times closer to its star than Mercury is to our Sun!

55 CANCRI E

ALPHA CENTAURI BB

1200 °C

The exoplanet named Alpha Centauri Bb has a surface temperature of around **1200 °C**, **which is almost three times hotter than Venus.**

VENUS

X3

AN EXOPLANET SYSTEM CALLED TRAPPIST-1
has 7 rocky planets going around its star. The planet system is about 40 light-years from Earth, in the constellation Aquarius.

Too warm

Just right for life!

Too cold

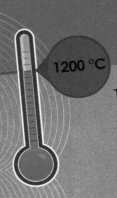

The Trappist planets are all **a similar size to Earth.**

Some have **WATER!**

THE OUTER PLANETS

URANUS

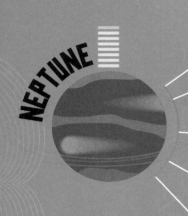

Radius = **25,362 km**

Distance from Sun = **2,871,000,000 km**

Time to orbit the Sun = **30,687 Earth days**

Rotation period = **17 hours**

Satellites (moons) = **27**

NEPTUNE

Radius = **24,622 km**

Distance from Sun = **4,499,000,000 km**

Time to orbit the Sun = **60,190 Earth days**

Rotation period = **16 hours**

Satellites (moons) = **14**

RINGS

JUPITER

SATURN

NEPTUNE

URANUS

30 kg = 71 kg

GRAVITY is different on each planet.

For example, if you weigh 30 kg on Earth, then your weight on Jupiter will be 71 kg!

SATURN

Radius = **58,232 km**

Distance from Sun
= **1,433,000,000 km**

Time to orbit the Sun
= **10,756 Earth days**

Rotation period
= **10.5 hours**

Satellites (moons) = **62**

Relative size of **Earth**

JUPITER

Radius = **69,911 km**

Distance from Sun
= **778,500,000 km**

Time to orbit the Sun
= **4,333 Earth days**

Rotation period
= **10 hours**

Satellites (moons) = **67**

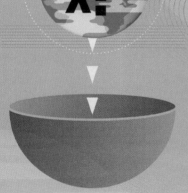

HOW MANY EARTHS FIT INSIDE?

Jupiter – **1,321**

Saturn – **763**

Uranus – **63**

Neptune – **57**

WIND SPEED

JUPITER
635 km/h

SATURN
1,800 km/h

URANUS
900 km/h

NEPTUNE
2,100 km/h

In comparison, the maximum wind speeds
reached (briefly) inside a tornado or powerful
hurricane on Earth is about 300 km/h.

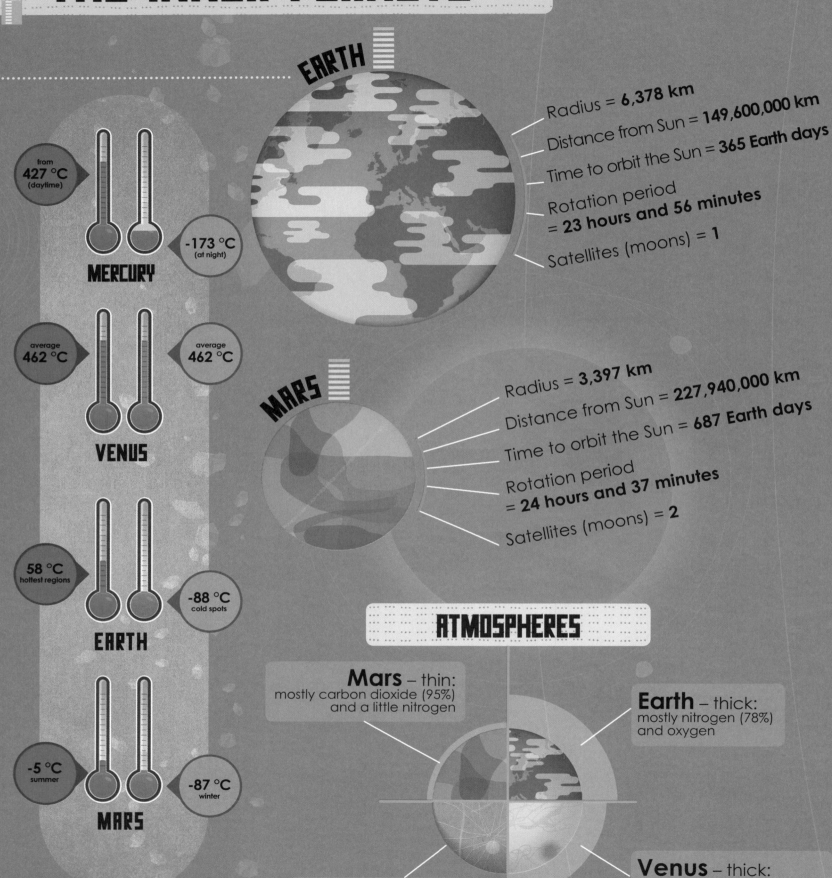

THE INNER PLANETS

MERCURY
from **427 °C** (daytime)
-173 °C (at night)

VENUS
average **462 °C**
average **462 °C**

EARTH
58 °C hottest regions
-88 °C cold spots

MARS
-5 °C summer
-87 °C winter

EARTH

Radius = **6,378 km**

Distance from Sun = **149,600,000 km**

Time to orbit the Sun = **365 Earth days**

Rotation period = **23 hours and 56 minutes**

Satellites (moons) = **1**

MARS

Radius = **3,397 km**

Distance from Sun = **227,940,000 km**

Time to orbit the Sun = **687 Earth days**

Rotation period = **24 hours and 37 minutes**

Satellites (moons) = **2**

ATMOSPHERES

Mars – thin: mostly carbon dioxide (95%) and a little nitrogen

Earth – thick: mostly nitrogen (78%) and oxygen

Mercury – none

Venus – thick: mostly carbon dioxide (98%), and a little nitrogen and sulphuric acid

MERCURY

Radius = **2,439 km**

Distance from Sun = **57,910,000 km**

Time to orbit the Sun = **88 Earth days**

Rotation period = **59 Earth days**

Satellites (moons) = **0**

VENUS

Radius = **6,052 km**

Distance from Sun = **108,200,000 km**

Time to orbit the Sun = **225 Earth days**

Rotation period = **243 Earth days**

Satellites (moons) = **0**

GIANT MOUNTAIN

Olympus Mons on Mars is the largest mountain in the solar system. It is nearly 25 km high – nearly three times the height of Mount Everest.

Olympus Mons

Mount Everest

WEATHER FORECASTS

MERCURY
No storms, cloud, wind or rain. Watch out for a huge drop in temperature from day to night!

VENUS
Total unbroken cloud cover from horizon to horizon. Crushing pressure and incredibly hot. Chance of acid rain in the clouds, but it won't reach the ground!

EARTH
Anything is possible: rain, storms, wind, clouds or sunshine.

MARS
Occasional light winds, but chance of huge dust storms that may turn the air orange!

OUR NEAREST STAR

CHROMOSPHERE
2,000 km thick
The outer layer of the
Sun's atmosphere.

PHOTOSPHERE
500 km thick
Energy radiates through here.

CONVECTIVE ZONE
200,000 km thick
Flowing currents of gas
carry energy to the outside
of the Sun's atmosphere.

RADIATIVE ZONE
350,000 km thick
The visible surface of the Sun.

CORE
150,000 km radius
The Sun's nuclear energy
is generated here.

5,500 °C surface temperature

1.3 million Earths
would fit inside the Sun

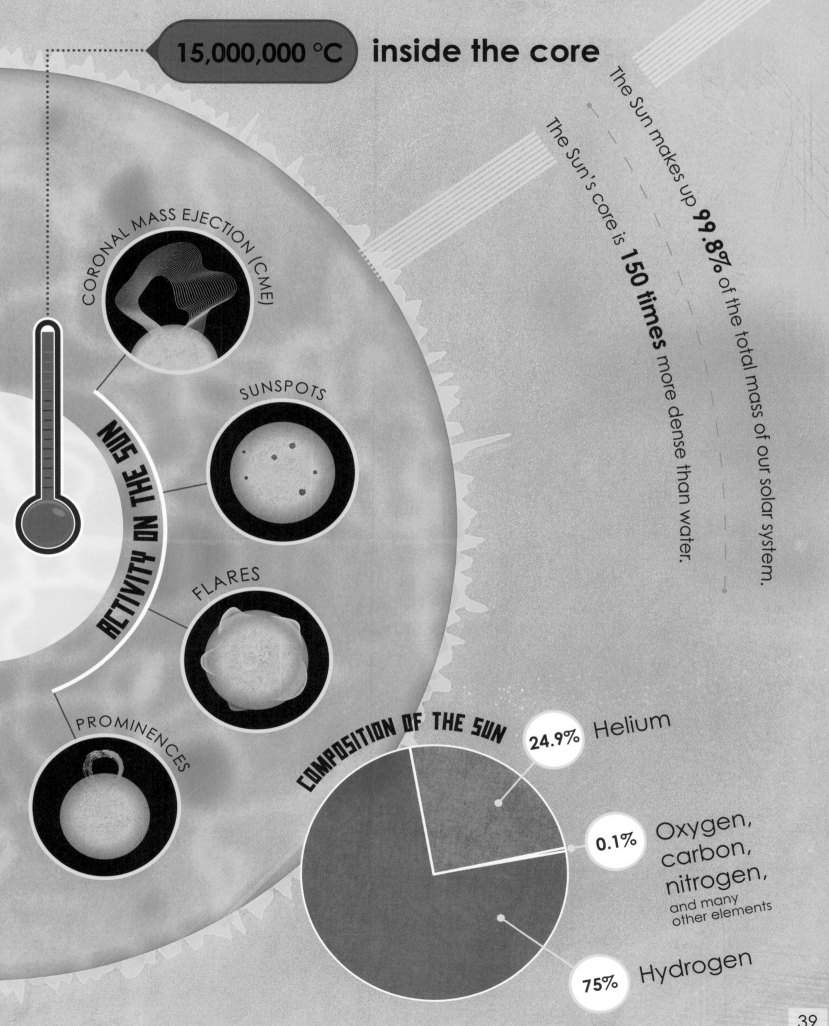

15,000,000 °C inside the core

The Sun makes up **99.8%** of the total mass of our solar system.

The Sun's core is **150 times** more dense than water.

ACTIVITY ON THE SUN

CORONAL MASS EJECTION (CME)

SUNSPOTS

FLARES

PROMINENCES

COMPOSITION OF THE SUN

24.9% Helium

0.1% Oxygen, carbon, nitrogen, and many other elements

75% Hydrogen

ORBITING EARTH

ISS has more **living space** than a 6-bed house.

Its speed in orbit is
27,760 km/h -
that means the ISS travels
a total distance each
day that is almost
the same as going to
the Moon and back!

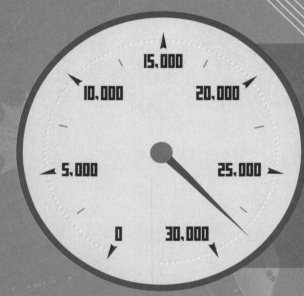

ISS weighs more than 320 cars!

The different crews
of astronauts on board
the ISS have eaten
a total of more than

25,000 meals so far.

52 computers
are used to
control the ISS.

There are more than
13 km of wires
for providing electricity to the ISS.

USA, Russia, Canada, Japan, Brazil, Belgium, Denmark,
France, Germany, Italy, the Netherlands, Norway,
Spain, Sweden, Switzerland and the United Kingdom **ALL CONTRIBUTE TO THE ISS.**

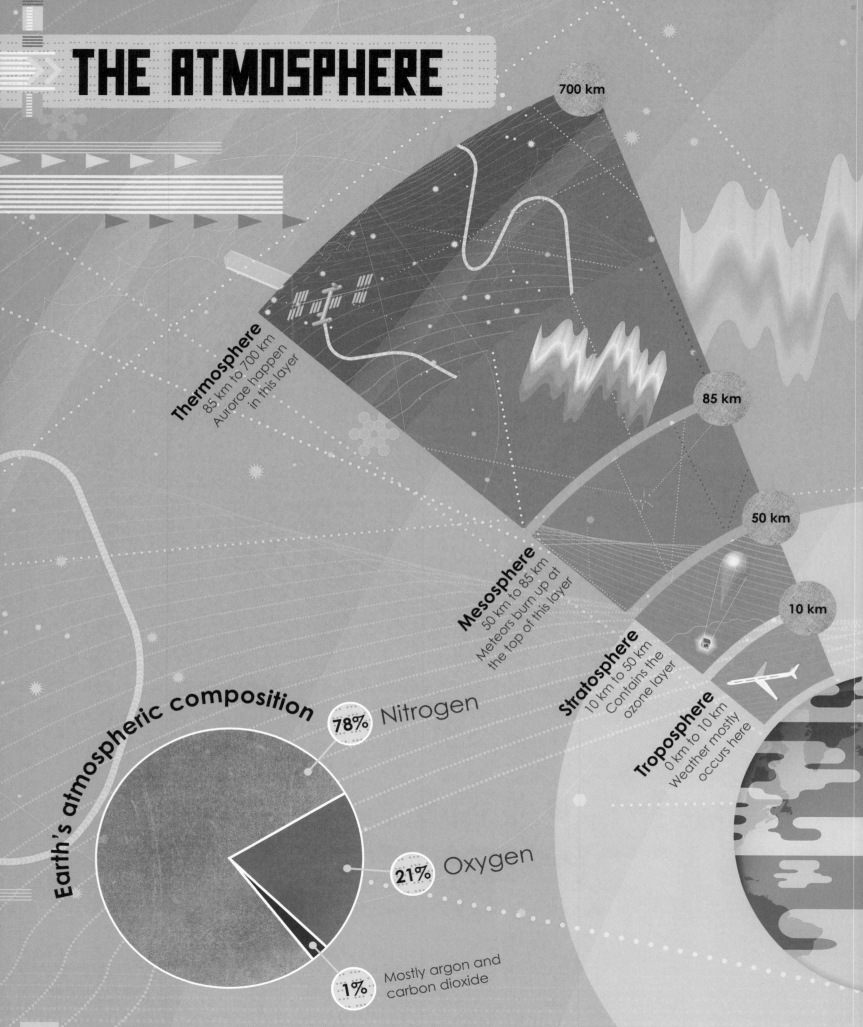

THE ATMOSPHERE

700 km

Thermosphere
85 km to 700 km
Aurorae happen
in this layer

85 km

50 km

Mesosphere
50 km to 85 km
Meteors burn up at
the top of this layer

10 km

Stratosphere
10 km to 50 km
Contains the
ozone layer

Troposphere
0 km to 10 km
Weather mostly
occurs here

Earth's atmospheric composition

78% Nitrogen

21% Oxygen

1% Mostly argon and
carbon dioxide

GREENHOUSE EFFECT

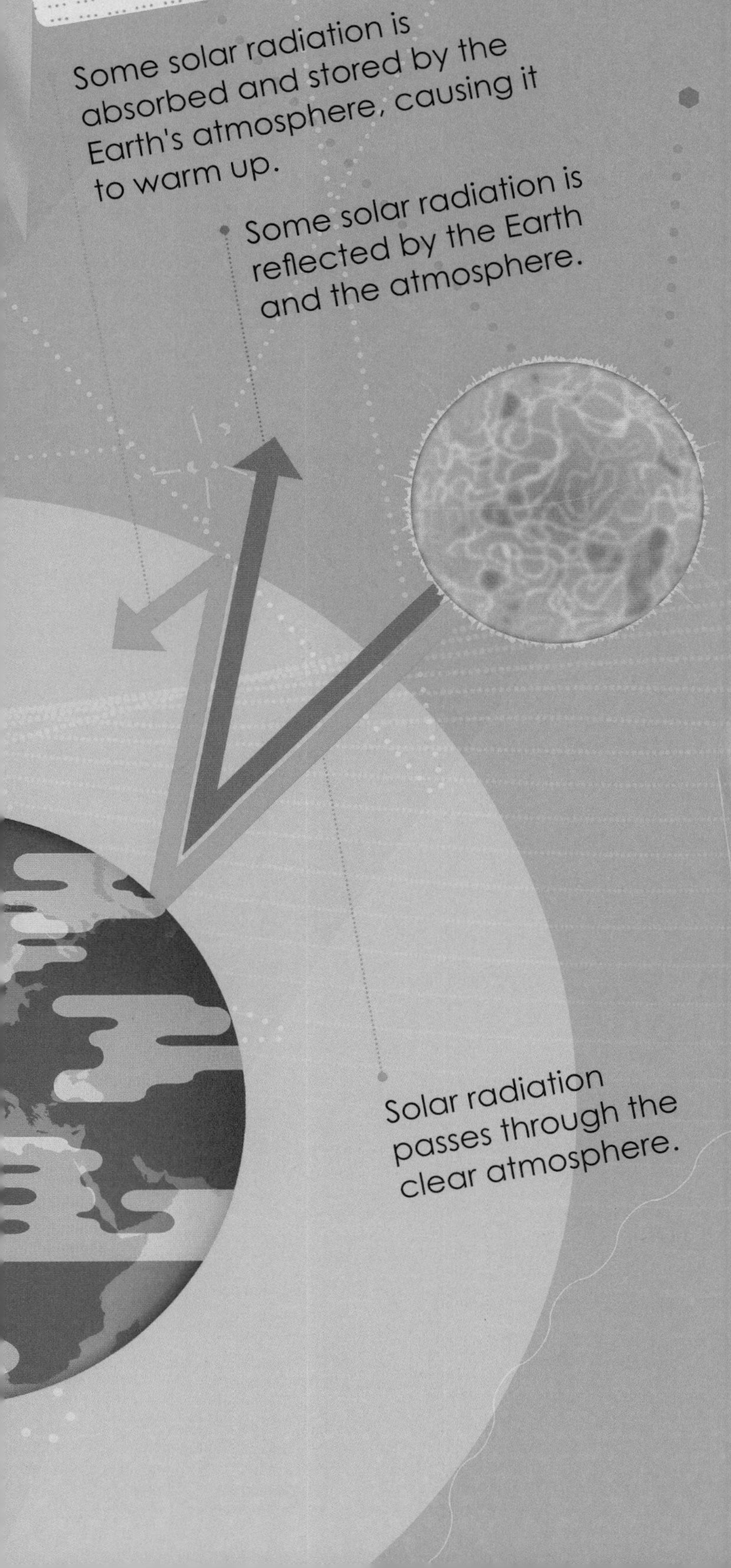

Some solar radiation is absorbed and stored by the Earth's atmosphere, causing it to warm up.

Some solar radiation is reflected by the Earth and the atmosphere.

Solar radiation passes through the clear atmosphere.

CLOUD TYPES IN THE TROPOSPHERE

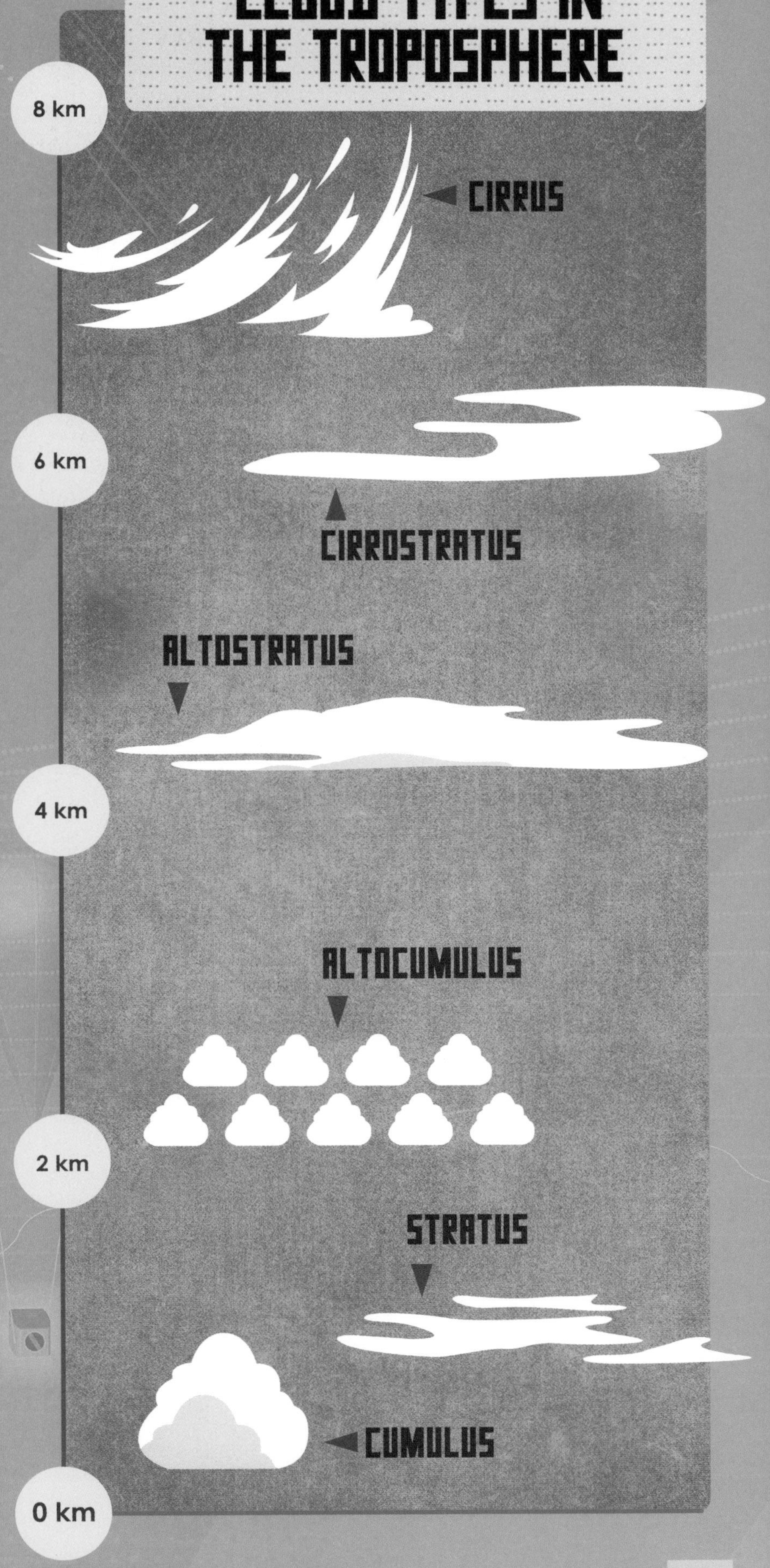

8 km

◄ CIRRUS

6 km

▲ CIRROSTRATUS

ALTOSTRATUS
▼

4 km

ALTOCUMULUS
▼

2 km

STRATUS
▼

0 km

◄ CUMULUS

!

Earth's inner core is 6,000 °C HOT.

That's hotter than the surface of the Sun!

CRUST
30–50 km thick

MANTLE
2,900 km thick

LIQUID OUTER CORE
2,250 km thick

SOLID INNER CORE
1,200 km thick

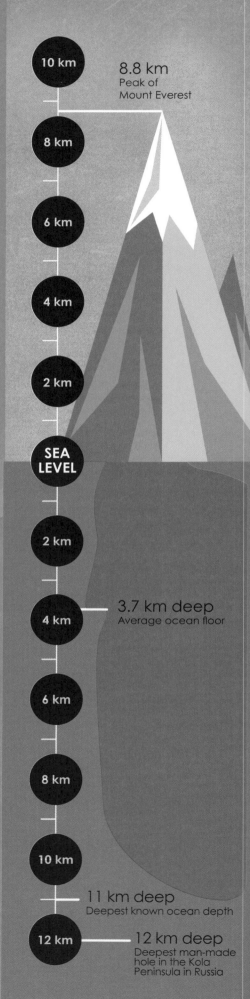

10 km

8.8 km
Peak of Mount Everest

8 km

6 km

4 km

2 km

SEA LEVEL

2 km

4 km
3.7 km deep
Average ocean floor

6 km

8 km

10 km

11 km deep
Deepest known ocean depth

12 km
12 km deep
Deepest man-made hole in the Kola Peninsula in Russia

PACIFIC OCEAN

Almost 645 million cubic km

ATLANTIC OCEAN

Almost 310 million cubic km

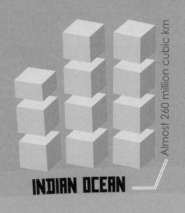

INDIAN OCEAN

Almost 260 million cubic km

FRESH WATER

Almost 35 million cubic km

About **70%** of the Earth's surface is covered in WATER.

Most of this is salt water in oceans.

There are about
9 million different
LIFE FORMS on Earth

INSECTS 5,000,000

ARACHNIDS 600,000

REPTILES 10,000

BIRDS 10,000

FISHES 40,000

MAMMALS 5,500

FLOWERING PLANTS 350,000

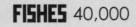

Every atom
around you
(and inside you)
was made by
the Big Bang
or by stars.
We are all
made of
stardust!

TIMELINE OF SPACE EXPLORATION

3 FEBRUARY
LUNA 9
First unmanned probe to land on the Moon

1956 | 1957 | 1958 | 1959 | 1960 | 1961 | 1962 | 1963 | 1964 | 1965 | 1966 | 1967 | 1968

4 OCTOBER
SPUTNIK 1
First artificial satellite in space

3 NOVEMBER
SPUTNIK 2
First live animal (Laika the dog) in space

SEPT–OCT
LUNA missions
First probes to the Moon

12 APRIL
VOSTOK 1
Yuri Gagarin is the first man into space

16 JUNE
Valentina Tereshkova is the first woman in space

18 MARCH
First spacewalk

JULY
MARINER 4
First close-up views of Mars

OCTOBER
VENERA 4
First probe to Venus

JANUARY
VOYAGER 2
arrives at Uranus

24 APRIL
HUBBLE SPACE TELESCOPE
launched

1982 | 1983 | 1984 | 1985 | 1986 | 1987 | 1988 | 1989 | 1990 | 1991 | 1992 | 1993 | 1994

1 MARCH
VENERA 2
lands on Venus

20 FEBRUARY
MIR SPACE STATION
launched

10 AUGUST
MAGELLAN
spacecraft arrives at Venus

25 AUGUST
VOYAGER 2
arrives at Neptune

6 AUGUST
CURIOSITY
rover lands on Mars

JANUARY
NEW HORIZONS
flyby of Pluto

2008 | 2009 | 2010 | 2011 | 2012 | 2013 | 2014 | 2015 | 2016 | 2017 | 2018 | 2019 | 2020

MARCH
MESSENGER
First spacecraft to orbit Mercury

AUGUST
First spacecraft to orbit a comet (Churyumov-Gerasimenko)

MARCH
DAWN
First spacecraft to orbit a dwarf planet (Ceres)

MARCH–JUNE
Planned launch of JAMES WEBB SPACE TELESCOPE – follow-up to the HUBBLE SPACE TELESCOPE

JULY
DAWN
spacecraft goes into orbit around asteroid Vesta

AUGUST
VOYAGER 1
crosses into interstellar space

12 NOVEMBER
PHILAE probe
lands on a comet

OCTOBER
Planned launch of BEPICOLOMBO mission to orbit Mercury

17 NOVEMBER
LUNOKHOD 1
First unmanned rover on the Moon

MAY
SKYLAB
First space station starts being built

AUG–SEPT
VOYAGER 1 and 2
First spacecraft launched to outer solar system

12 APRIL
First **SPACE SHUTTLE** launch

1969 | 1970 | 1971 | 1972 | 1973 | 1974 | 1975 | 1976 | 1977 | 1978 | 1979 | 1980 | 1981

20 JULY
APOLLO 11
Neil Armstrong
First man to walk on the Moon

DECEMBER
APOLLO 17
Last human mission to the Moon

MARCH
MARINER 10
First spacecraft fly-by of Mercury

20 JULY
VIKING 1
First pictures from the surface of Mars

25 AUGUST
VOYAGER 2
arrives at Saturn

15 DECEMBER
VENERA 7
First probe to soft-land on the surface of Venus

20 NOVEMBER
Launch of the first **ISS MODULE**

FEBRUARY
NEAR SHOEMAKER
First spacecraft to orbit an asteroid (*Eros*)

NOVEMBER
VOYAGER 1
arrives at Saturn

AUGUST
SPRITZER SPACE TELESCOPE
launched

1995 | 1996 | 1997 | 1998 | 1999 | 2000 | 2001 | 2002 | 2003 | 2004 | 2005 | 2006 | 2007

DECEMBER
GALILEO
arrives at Jupiter

4 JULY
PATHFINDER
rover lands on Mars

SEPTEMBER
CHANDRA X-RAY OBSERVATORY
launched

12 FEBRUARY
NEAR SHOEMAKER
makes first landing on an asteroid

DECEMBER
MARS EXPRESS
goes into orbit around Mars

14 JANUARY
HUYGENS probe lands on Saturn's moon Titan

DECEMBER
SOHO
Solar observatory launched

SEPTEMBER
MARS GLOBAL SURVEYOR
goes into orbit around Mars

28 APRIL
First tourist in space

JANUARY
SPIRIT and **OPPORTUNITY**
rovers land on Mars

30 JUNE
CASSINI
spacecraft arrives at Saturn

MARCH
MARS RECONNAISSANCE ORBITER goes into orbit around Mars

2021 | 2022 | 2023 | 2024 | 2025 | 2026 | 2027 | 2028 | 2029 | 2030 | 2031 | 2032 | 2033

NASA due to launch **LUCY** mission to study Trojan asteroids close to the orbit of Jupiter

Planned launch of **JUICE** to explore the icy moons of Jupiter

Launch of **ESA PLATO** spacecraft mission to study rocky exoplanets

Possible first manned mission to Mars

Proposed launch for Russia's **MERCURY-P** spacecraft, which will perform the first ever landing on Mercury

GLOSSARY

asteroid: a medium-sized rocky object, also known as a planetoid, that orbits (circles) the Sun. Most asteroids are in the asteroid belt between Mars and Jupiter.

astronomy: the study of the stars, planets and other bodies (eg: comets, meteors) in space.

atmosphere: the layer of gases that surrounds a planet.

atom: the smallest part of an element or substance.

axis: an imaginary line around which an object rotates.

black hole: an object in space, which has such a strong gravitational pull that it sucks in anything around it, even light, so it appears black.

celestial: relating to the sky or the heavens. Stars and planets are celestial bodies.

comet: a giant frozen ball of gas and dust that travels around the Sun. When the comet gets near to the Sun, some of the ice melts and leaves a dusty trail behind the ball that looks like a tail.

constellation: a group of stars in the night sky, that make a shape if you join them with imaginary lines like a dot-to-dot.

cosmology: a branch of astronomy that looks at the origin, structure and development of the Universe.

dark energy: a form of energy that makes up about three-quarters of the mass of the Universe's energy, and which produces a force that pulls in the opposite direction to gravity, making the Universe expand.

dark matter: ordinary matter, like planets or stars, is made up of atoms. Only about 15% of the matter in the Universe is made of atoms. The rest, called dark matter, is invisible, and can only be detected by its gravitational (its pull) effects on ordinary matter.

diverse multitude: a large and varied number of people and creatures.

dwarf planet: a planet-like object that orbits the Sun and is big enough to have become round-shaped by its own force of gravity, but has not cleared its orbital path of other space objects.

eclipse: the shadow caused by one celestial body (eg: moon) blocking the light from another (eg: the Sun).

ellipse: an oval shape like a flattened circle.

galaxy: a large group of stars. Our galaxy (called the Milky Way) includes the Sun.

gravity: the natural force of attraction that pulls objects together. It pulls all objects near Earth towards it, giving them weight. This is what keeps our feet on the ground.

interstellar: situated or occurring between the stars.

mass: the actual amount of matter that is contained in an object.

matter: anything that has mass and occupies space.

meteor: a small piece of space rock or dust that burns up as it enters the Earth's atmosphere, producing a streak of light.

meteorite: a part of a meteoroid found on Earth. It reaches Earth without burning up in the atmosphere.

meteoroid: a small rock in space.

The Milky Way: our galaxy. It is spiral shaped and contains our Sun and solar system and hundreds of billions of stars.

orbit: the continuous movement of an object around a star or planet.

planet: an object bigger than an asteroid that orbits a star.

probe: a device that is used to gather information from outer space and send it back to Earth.

satellite: a device placed in orbit around the Earth or another planet that is used to collect information or for communication.

solar: relating to the Sun.

solar system: the Sun and the planets and their moons, that orbit the Sun.

sphere: a round object or a three-dimensional shape or object that looks like a ball.

star: any celestial body in space that is made of burning gas and that looks like a tiny point of light in the night sky.

supernova: the explosion of a very large star at the end of its life.

ultraviolet (UV) rays: light waves beyond the violet end of the spectrum of visible light.

Universe: the whole of space and everything (matter and energy) that it contains.

weight: the gravitational force that is pulling on an object.